PASS, CATCH, TACKLE
FOOTBALL VERBS

By Mark Weakland

CAPSTONE PRESS
a capstone imprint

A football soars into the air. Defensive players leap and stretch their arms, trying to block it. Football is a game of action, and that makes it a game of **verbs**. Action words, such as "soars," "leap," "stretch," and "block," are verbs. Turn the page and let's look for football verbs!

Verbs keep the football moving! A quarterback **passes** the ball to move it down the field. The most exciting pass is the long bomb. Raising his arm, the quarterback prepares to **hurl** the ball to a receiver downfield.

Receivers **catch** what the quarterback throws. To **snatch** the ball out of the air, receivers must have strong hands and quick reflexes. They also need great concentration. Keep your eyes on the ball! If this receiver **snags** the football, he'll score a touchdown for his team.

Run is an important football verb. In a football game, everyone runs. But only one position has the main job of running with the ball—the running back, of course! The defense rushes after the back, hoping to tackle him quickly. If he gets away, they'll have to chase after him!

Verbs can also stop the motion of the ball. The main job of the defensive players is to **tackle**. Defenders try to stop the person with the ball. To do this, defensive players **grab**, **drag**, and **pull** offensive players to the ground.

A great running back uses quick verbs to get around defenders. He **dodges** tacklers by running to the right and cutting left. He **jumps** through the arms of linebackers. Once a running back **escapes** the defense, he **sprints** down the field.

Action verbs make football plays come alive. Linebackers **plunge** forward to tackle the quarterback. Receivers **stretch** to catch the ball. Running backs **dive** toward the goal line. If the football crosses the line, it's a touchdown!

Leap and **jump** are both action verbs, but which verb is more exciting? When the ball is thrown over his head, a receiver leaps with his arms raised high. The defender jumps up to knock the ball away. But with a mighty stretch, the receiver makes the catch.

Special teams wouldn't be so special without verbs! After a kickoff or punt, the receiving team **returns** the ball. The player **positions** himself under the tumbling football. Once he catches the ball, he's off like a rabbit, **sprinting** full speed down the field.

Verbs are full of surprises. The defense **stuns** the offense when they **block** the punt. Defensive players **lunge** for the football as it leaves the punter's foot. If they **swat** the ball down, they might also **recover** it.

Verbs put points on the scoreboard! Passing and running can lead to a six-point touchdown, but some points are earned by **kicking**. A kicker **boots** the ball with a tremendous swing of his leg. The football **flies**, end-over-end, down the field and through the uprights. Three points!

23

Defensive players **storm** into the backfield, and the quarterback can't get away. He's hit hard as the linemen tackle him, and he **fumbles** the ball. That's one verb every quarterback dreads! Now the ball is loose. Which team will **grab** it?

Cheerleaders **cheer** their teams on from the sidelines. In college games, cheerleaders are men and women. They **energize** the crowd and bring fans to their feet. Cheerleaders **perform** all kinds of verbs during the game. They lift, balance, stretch, twirl, flip, tumble, and dance!

Football games explode with nonstop action—and action words! Can you find all the verbs used to describe the exciting action of this scoring play?

As linemen **block** the speedy defenders, a running back **stretches** for the goal line. One player **dives** at the running back, while another **grabs** his ankle.

Answer: block, stretches, dives, grabs

GLOSSARY

block (BLOK)—to keep an opponent from reaching the ball carrier

cheer (CHIHR)—to shout encouragement

dive (DIVE)—to lunge forward as you fall to the ground

dodge (DOJ)—to avoid something by moving quickly

fumble (FUHM-buhl)—to drop the football

leap (LEEP)—to jump high into the air

pass (PASS)—to throw a football

sprint (SPRINT)—to run fast for a short distance

tackle (TAK-uhl)—to stop another player by knocking him to the ground

verb (VURB)—a word that expresses an action

READ MORE

Blaisdell, Bette. *A Backpack Full of Verbs.* Words I Know. North Mankato, Minn.: Capstone Press, 2014.

Cleary, Brian. *Slide and Slurp, Scratch and Burp: More About Verbs.* Words are CATegorical. New York: Millbrook Press, 2009.

Walton, Rick. *Bullfrog Pops! An Adventure in Verbs and Direct Objects.* Layton, Utah: Gibbs Smith, 2011.

INTERNET SITES

FactHound offers a safe, fun way to find Internet sites related to this book. All of the sites on FactHound have been researched by our staff.

Here's all you do:

Visit *www.facthound.com*

Type in this code: 9781620651599

Super-cool **stuff!** Check out projects, games and lots more at **www.capstonekids.com**

INDEX

Sports Illustrated Kids Football Words are published by Capstone Press, 1710 Roe Crest Drive, North Mankato, Minnesota 56003
www.capstonepub.com

Library of Congress Cataloging-in-Publication Data
Cataloging-in-Publication data is on file with the Library of Congress.
ISBN 978-1-62065-159-9 (library binding)
ISBN 978-1-4914-7599-7 (eBook PDF)

Editorial Credits
Anthony Wacholtz, editor; Terri Poburka and Ted Williams, designers;
Eric Gohl, media researcher; Katy LaVigne, production specialist

Photo Credits
Sports Illustrated: Al Tielemans, 2–3, 18–19, 24–25, Bill Frakes, 20–21, Bob Rosato, 26–27, David E. Klutho, 4–5, John Biever, cover, 1, 12–13, John W. McDonough, 6–7, 8–9, 16–17, 28–29, Robert Beck, 14–15, 22–23, Simon Bruty, 10–11

Design Elements: Shutterstock

Printed in the United States of America in North Mankato, Minnesota.
032015   008823CGF15